What my parents taught me about sex, marriage & choosing a husband

Huey Cuffie
Petreece Cuffie

Table of Contents

For Joelle,
Our daughter.
You are God's gift to us, our pride and joy.
May the Lord always guide your steps,
blessing you with wisdom,
favour and a loving family.

Special Note to Young Women

We have written this book with our own daughter and young women in mind. We want our daughter Joelle to have a great future including a healthy and happy marriage. We want this for you as well. We appreciate the many challenges and fears you must overcome regarding relationships and choosing a husband. While some of you may be blessed with strong parental support and input, many others have had to struggle without this important resource. If for some reason you do not have access to parental wisdom, this book is especially for you. You are not alone and we hope this book will help you feel supported, encouraged and loved.

Finally, we have written the last chapter directly to your interested male friend or intended partner. We encourage you to let him read that chapter. Even better, let him read the entire book! In our years of counseling individuals and couples, we have discovered that the woman is likely to bear most of the burden for fixing an unhealthy relationship. Your influence on having a successful marriage is greatest BEFORE you get married. This is why you must seriously consider any of the warning signs raised in this book and respond accordingly.

Huey & Petreece Cuffie

November 2013

The 2 Most Important Decisions in Your Life

From your mother

D ear daughter,
You are so beautiful, trusting and willing to give. These attributes will serve you well in a world of pain and grief, if mixed with wisdom and love for self, God and man.

I remember feeling at times a great weight of responsibility when you were born. Like most parents, your daddy and I have sought to ensure that you are equipped to face the world as an adult with or without us.

Always know that no matter how you feel, you are beautiful, intelligent and loved by God. My experience as a woman, counsellor, friend and sister has taught me that your two most important decisions in life are:

1. Who you will serve as the Source of your life (spirituality) and

2. Who you will choose as your partner in life (marriage).

You already know that Jesus is your Source and you continue to know Him better and love Him more.

But this letter is not to address that relationship. It is to address the other decision.

This decision, involving the choice of a marriage partner, has left some women feeling like they are the most beautiful, treasured and blessed persons on earth, while many others spend sleepless nights wondering:

"What went wrong?"

"Am I too fat?"

"Does he have another lover?"

"Why does he not allow me to answer his phone?"

"Why don't we speak anymore?"

"Why won't he go out with me?"

"Am I being taken for granted?"

I want to give you some words of wisdom, some counsel, some guidelines. Where do I start? I will discuss some of the common mistakes women make that leave them with a lifetime of regret. There is an old saying that your grandmother used often as she tried to counsel young women on this important decision: "Marry in haste, repent in leisure."

This is harder to write than I expected. I remember the faces and issues of women in pain as I cried with some, prayed with others, while trying to help them all. It is my hope and fervent prayer that you will avoid such pain and misfortune by paying heed to my words and by following the example I have set for you.

I pray that the LORD will give you understanding as you read these pages. May our loving, heavenly Father grant you the ability to choose wisely so that one day when you are ready, you will say "I do" to a man who will love and cherish you all the days of your life… even as Christ loves His Church.

With all love and affection,

Mom

To forgive is to set a prisoner free and discover the prisoner was you.

- Author unknown[1]

Forgiveness

From your mother

L et's start with the man who can't forgive family members and past friends for the hurt they have caused in his life. I have heard people say, with pride, "I will never forgive him" or "she does not deserve my forgiveness." I get really scared when I hear those words especially in relation to family members and close friends.

Forgiveness is critical to a healthy marriage. You are not perfect. You will both make mistakes. You will hurt each other and sometimes badly and if both of you have not developed the ability to forgive and reconcile, your relationship will fall apart eventually.

Let me talk a little about forgiveness. Forgiveness is called a crisis of the will. We usually don't want to forgive. When we are hurt deeply or offended we usually want justice and that is normal. After all, we are created in the image of God and He is a just God. However, we don't know what a person justly deserves and we have all hurt others and are ourselves in need of forgiveness. We feel good to know that God forgives us, so it follows that we should forgive others.

Forgiveness does not mean forgetting because the

human mind does not forget painful experiences especially where relationships are concerned. We can repress them but we don't forget them. If those painful feelings with regard to people are not healed through forgiveness, they will affect the ability of a person to communicate and to be intimate (i.e. To give and receive love).

Forgiveness does not always lead to reconciliation (restoration of the relationship) but it is a major first step. When you forgive, your pain is healed and it gives you the ability to avoid generalising about people and carrying "trust issues" around. No doubt you have heard some women declare in bitterness that they will never trust a man again or the classic "All men are dogs!" Such statements usually result from hurt they experienced in previous relationships. This hurt can act as a barrier to healthy relationships in the future. Forgiveness, in effect, frees you to continue to have healthy relationships with people.

When you forgive it does not necessarily change the other person. So in circumstances where the other person is not willing to change, you will need to adjust your interaction with them to avoid further hurt.

We should however seek reconciliation where possible and in a marriage it is absolutely necessary. Forgiveness and reconciliation in marriage actually leads to positive growth and enrichment of your marriage. It strengthens your love and appreciation for others. If he cannot forgive his close friends and family it will be very difficult for him to forgive you. People closest to us can cause the most hurt because of the nature of the relationship. It is therefore important to determine if he has a track record of forgiving friends and family.

Don't marry a man who cannot say, "I forgive you." Don't marry a man who cannot say, "I am sorry, please forgive me." This marriage will be very painful and lonely.

With all love and affection,

Mom

Daddy's point of view

Your mother and I have a wonderful marriage but there are times when we disagree or argue. During those moments, one can get very emotional and say some hurtful things. The more comfortable you are around a person, the more likely you are to express negative thoughts and feelings when you're angry.

Our ability to forgive one another is a crucial part of our marriage. I know close hand the destructive power of condemnation and when we withhold forgiveness from our spouses, they become vulnerable to condemnation's poison. So while I may hurt from the offense, I hurt more from the thought of my wife suffering from the anguish of guilt and condemnation. Withholding forgiveness from your partner "until he deserves it" or "until his probation is over," is not wise. Unforgiveness gives the devil space to work his dark mischief.

Having been born out of wedlock and my parents not being there for me when I was young, made me feel angry and rejected. The pain was so real that I made a vow that I would not have children before I was married. I did not want to make the same mistakes my parents made. But the Holy Spirit gently warned me that if I did not forgive my parents I would be in danger of doing the very same thing they did - and worse! I then thought about young men who hated their alcoholic fathers only to become alcoholics themselves or sons who vowed never to hit their wives, as their fathers did, but then were horrified after striking their spouses. You see forgiveness not only heals, it breaks the vicious cycle of pain that threatens to continue into the next generation. So I learned to forgive and though it was painful, it was necessary if I wanted to thrive as a man and keep that vow I made concerning you.

It's helpful to remember that your mother has willingly forgiven me for the countless mistakes I have made. This too gives me the strength to forgive and to ask for forgiveness. Forgiveness is the secret ingredient in successful marriages. Make sure both you and your future husband have plenty of it.

Love always,

Dad

Things to Consider Before You Get Married

1. Read the Scriptures in the following section together and discuss.

2. Ask your boyfriend/ fiancé his views on forgiveness. When is forgiveness deserved? Are there any circumstances in which forgiveness should be withheld?

3. Ask your boyfriend/ fiancé to share an experience where he hurt someone and asked for forgiveness.

4. Ask your boyfriend/ fiancé to share a time when someone close to him hurt him. Has he forgiven the person? How does he feel towards the person?

What the Bible Says...

Get rid of all bitterness, rage, anger, harsh words, and slander, as well as all types of evil behavior. Instead, be kind to each other, tenderhearted, forgiving one another, just as God through Christ has forgiven you.

Ephesians 4:31, 32, NLT

Make allowance for each other's faults, and forgive anyone who offends you. Remember, the Lord forgave you, so you must forgive others.

Colossians 3:13, NLT

Then Peter came to him and asked, "Lord, how often should I forgive someone who sins against me? Seven times?"

"No, not seven times," Jesus replied, "but seventy times seven!

"Therefore, the Kingdom of Heaven can be compared to a king who decided to bring his accounts up to date with servants who had borrowed money from him. In the process, one of his debtors was brought in who owed him millions of dollars. He couldn't pay, so his master ordered that he be sold—along with his wife, his children, and everything he owned—to pay the debt.

"But the man fell down before his master and begged him, 'Please, be patient with me, and I will pay it all.' Then his master was filled with pity for him, and he released him and forgave his debt.

"But when the man left the king, he went to a fellow servant who owed him a few thousand dollars. He grabbed him by the throat and demanded instant payment.

"His fellow servant fell down before him and begged for a little more time. 'Be patient with me, and I will pay it,' he pleaded. But his creditor wouldn't wait. He had the man arrested and put in prison until the debt could be paid in full.

"When some of the other servants saw this, they were very upset. They went to the king and told him everything that had happened. Then the king called in the man he had forgiven and said, 'You evil servant! I forgave you that tremendous debt because you pleaded with me. Shouldn't you have mercy on your fellow servant, just as I had mercy on you?' Then the angry king sent the man to prison to be tortured until he had paid his entire debt.

"That's what my heavenly Father will do to you if you refuse to forgive your brothers and sisters from your heart."

Matthew 18:21 – 35, NLT

One day Jesus said to his disciples, "There will always be temptations to sin, but what sorrow awaits the person who does the tempting! It would be better to be thrown into the sea with a millstone hung around your neck than to cause one of these little ones to fall into sin. So watch yourselves!

"If another believer sins, rebuke that person; then if there is repentance, forgive. Even if that person wrongs you seven times a day and each time turns again and asks forgiveness, you must forgive."

Luke 17:1 – 4, NLT

Your Notes...

It is the peculiar quality of a fool to perceive the faults of others and to forget his own.

The greatest of all faults is to be conscious of none.

- Thomas Carlyle [2]

Beware the Blamer

From your mother

Honey, we human beings have a long history of blaming others dating back to the Garden of Eden. Adam blamed Eve and Eve in turn blamed Satan for sinning against God.

The problem with blaming is that we miss important lessons that would lead to attitude and character development. Also in the act blaming others, we make ourselves the victim - a person without choice. You do not want to be a victim.

As children, we have little or no say in a lot of the things that come our way; we are "victims". As adults however, we can decide how we respond to circumstances and people. If you say, "I hit him because he made me angry..." people may understand your actions but him making you angry is not the reason for you hitting him. You had other choices - your hitting him is not his fault. If you believed that you had no other choice and what you did was right, then you are a victim to situations and circumstances and positive growth cannot take place.

A blamer can find real or imagined people and situations to justify his actions. This means there is no need for him to evaluate his actions, decisions and thinking. There is no need for him to change... only you and others.

When a person marries a blamer she can sometimes feel she's going crazy! This has a lot to do with the fact that as a woman you have a great desire to please and serve your husband. When he blames you for all or most of his discomfort, problems or failings in the relationship, it will eventually eat away at your ability to see yourself as a capable and intelligent person. It undermines your sense of self and you feel off-balanced.

Listen carefully to what he has to say about past failed relationships. Is it always someone else's fault? What has he learnt about himself as a result of the failures? What could he have done differently? What is he now willing to do differently? These are important questions. You must know the answers.

I hope what I'm writing is not overwhelming you but I will like you to read my entire letter and probably read it a second time. Share what I write with your friends as well because some of us have no one to guide us.

With all love and affection,
Mom

Daddy's point of view

No one is perfect. We all make mistakes. Yet it takes a real man to admit his shortcomings. I have discovered that only strong and secure men can come to terms with their failures. We are not talking here about those men who take delight in highlighting their weaknesses so they can be pitied or excused. No, the men I speak of see confession as a path to wholeness and recovery. They draw strength from the fact that they can choose their response; that they alone are responsible for their choices, for better or worse. They are not victims. They are conquerors. This is the kind of man you want to marry.

Consider King David who despite his royal position owned up to his numerous failures when confronted by God's prophets. For example he accepted that he was responsible for his sin of adultery with Bathsheba. His prayer of contrition is found in Psalms 32 and 51. I have meditated on these portions of Scriptures countless times when I myself have sinned whether against God or man. Confession frees us from the increasing burden of guilt. To hide our sin, to justify our mistakes, to deflect our shortcomings unto others, turns us into something weaker, ugly. Blamers do not grow because they do not learn about themselves. They are always right, never wrong. They think themselves always well while others are sick. You do not want to marry a blamer.

Love always,

Dad

Things to Consider Before You Get Married

1. Commit together to establish a Blame-Free culture within your relationship. Determine to seek out the log you may have in your own eye i.e. "What am I contributing to the problem?" Trust God to help your partner to recognize their part in the problem.

2. Make it easy for each other to admit when they are wrong. Don't rub it in. Avoid reminding your partner of past mistakes or failures during new conflicts.

3. Rather than taking a blame finding approach to your problems, adopt a problem-solving approach characterized by the questions, "What can we learn from this?" or "How can we deal with this together?"

What the Bible Says...

Oh, what joy for those

    whose disobedience is forgiven,

    whose sin is put out of sight!

  Yes, what joy for those

    whose record the Lord has cleared of guilt,

    whose lives are lived in complete honesty!

When I refused to confess my sin,

    my body wasted away,

    and I groaned all day long.

  Day and night your hand of discipline was heavy on me.

    My strength evaporated like water in the summer heat.

  Finally, I confessed all my sins to you

    and stopped trying to hide my guilt.

  I said to myself, "I will confess my rebellion to the Lord."

    And you forgave me! All my guilt is gone.

Psalms 32: 1 – 5, NLT

"And why worry about a speck in your friend's eye when you have a log in your own? How can you think of saying to your friend, 'Let me help you get rid of that speck in your eye,' when you can't see past the log in your own eye? Hypocrite! First get rid of the log in your own eye; then you will see well enough to deal with the speck in your friend's eye."

Matthew 7: 3 – 5, NLT

"When he finally came to his senses, he said to himself, 'At home even the hired servants have food enough to spare, and here I am dying of hunger! I will go home to my father and say, "Father, I have sinned against both heaven and you, and I am no longer worthy of being called your son. Please take me on as a hired servant."'

"So he returned home to his father. And while he was still a long way off, his father saw him coming. Filled with love and compassion, he ran to his son, embraced him, and kissed him. His son said to him, 'Father, I have sinned against both heaven and you, and I am no longer worthy of being called your son.'

"But his father said to the servants, 'Quick! Bring the finest robe in the house and put it on him. Get a ring for his finger and sandals for his feet.

Luke 15: 17 – 22, NLT

Confess your sins to each other and pray for each other so that you may be healed. The earnest prayer of a righteous person has great power and produces wonderful results.

James 5:16, NLT

If you ignore criticism, you will end in poverty and disgrace;

if you accept correction, you will be honored.

Proverbs 13: 18, NLT

Your Notes...

Within marriage, sex is beautiful, fulfilling, creative. Outside of marriage, it is ugly, destructive, and damning.

- John MacArthur [3]

Sex Before Marriage

From your mother

N ow concerning the issue of sex before marriage. Your father and I have taught you that God, the Creator of all things, has designed sex to be expressed and enjoyed only within the boundaries of marriage. Many people know this and some believe this.

I just want to give some time to explaining the importance of this to the stability and wholeness of your marriage. All of God's laws if followed protect us. They protect us from severe consequences that our human minds could never foresee. They also enable us to fully enjoy all of God's blessings. Sex is one of these blessings.

Abstaining from premarital sex helps you to know the other person better. Once premarital sex takes place, your relationship becomes driven by sexual passion rather than the healthy desire to know the person. It also gets in the way of showing concern for the other person's wellbeing. So no longer is it about having a good time with friends and family as we grow in knowledge and love for each other. Your relationship now deteriorates into a frantic when-and-where-can-we-meet-next-to-make-out mission. The relationship now revolves around this and knowing each other in a deep and real way takes a backseat.

Decisions about the relationship are then made based on feelings of passion and not on knowledge, wisdom, truth and principles. I have heard many couples before marriage say "you would never understand how strong our love is." only to see them 4-5 years later separated or divorced.

There is a saying, "Come see me and come live with me are two different things!" This generally happens because one of the persons (or both persons) was not being honest about their feelings and views on issues or time was not spent to really know the person, his views, family interactions, beliefs and emotional capacity. This happened because the couple was consumed with passion rather than sober judgment.

There is a discipline we develop in being able to say no to sexual activity with someone we have intense feelings and attraction for and to whom we are not yet married. This discipline will safeguard your marriage. You may wonder how.

Just because you are married does not mean there will not be people you are attracted to or who are attracted to you. By developing this discipline to say no before marriage both of you will have the discipline after marriage to also say no and safeguard your marriage.

Don't believe the myth "If you love me you will have sex with me." If someone loves you he will respect your values (and hopefully have similar values) and he will be willing to wait. He will love you, the person, enough to wait, knowing that his wait would not be in vain.

You may also hear the question, "We will get married anyway, so why wait?" Well, you don't know that you will get married until you say "I do." There are many women who fall for this trick and are waiting for many years now. This also puts "pressure" on the young woman who may believe strongly that she should marry the man she has sexual relations with and therefore would stay in a relationship despite all the negatives. She wants to believe him because he said "it's ok to have sex because I will marry you."

Remember however that premarital sex is not the "unpardonable sin." God can and will forgive this sin and heal the guilt and shame. If you are involved in premarital sex, you can stop – it will be difficult but it is not impossible. Get the help of God and mature, confidential persons. Stop before you get married so both of you can develop the discipline of saying no to sexual relations with someone who is not your spouse. You will safeguard your marriage in the future.

Stop – so you can get to know the real person in the relationship.

Stop – so you can learn to communicate and interact with each other in a healthy way.

Stop – to allow true love to grow and blossom.

With all love and affection,

Mom

Daddy's point of view

Your mother is a beautiful woman. I think that is where you get your looks. I have always been attracted to her and this no doubt presented one of our greatest challenges. You feel physically drawn to each other and you have to consciously resist going beyond established boundaries.

I am happy to say that we were virgins when we got married but it was not easy. Kissing and touching were major sources of stress. Sometimes it is these so-called gray areas that threaten sexual purity in relationships. Your mother and I both agreed to avoid such behaviours because we knew it could go into dangerous territory. We knew our limitations and were not afraid to admit them. Many premarital couples have compromised their sexual purity because they underestimated the power of sexual attraction.

You can avoid this by discussing the reality and dangers of sexual temptation. Share your intention to honour the values we have taught you, with your boyfriend/ fiancé. Develop mutually agreed strategies for minimizing sexual temptation and ask the LORD to keep both of you sexually pure for your future spouse. Having similar values can be an advantage whereas dissimilar standards concerning sexually intimacy before marriage can be an incredible emotional and spiritual strain. It is also tremendously helpful when you make yourself accountable to a mature and trusted couple.

Men seem more vulnerable to sexual temptation than women. I sought to counter this vulnerability by recognizing that until I married your mother, she was only my sister. It was quite possible that she may marry someone else. This gave me focus and a sense of responsibility for your mother's purity. Perspective is important and when a man sees a woman as a sister, certain temptations are minimized. A brother's perspective is beautifully illustrated in the following Scripture:

"We have a little sister

too young to have breasts.

What will we do for our sister

If someone asks to marry her?

If she is a virgin, like a wall,

We will protect her with a silver tower.

But if she is promiscuous, like a swinging door,

We will block her door with a cedar bar."

Song of Songs 8: 8,9, NLT

I strongly believe that women must challenge men to sexual purity. A weak brother can develop discipline when it becomes pretty clear to him that he will lose his love interest if he persists in unacceptable behaviour. Don't worry, your husband, the man worth marrying will consider you worth waiting for. As your mother and I would say to encourage each other to stand when the pressure felt strong, "later would be greater."

Love always,

Dad

Things to Consider Before You Get Married

1. Have a candid yet appropriate discussion on intimacy in your relationship. Share your values and standards with your intended partner. Be sure to find out what he thinks about premarital sex and his attitude towards the gray areas of physical intimacy.

2. Together, develop and commit beforehand to strategies for minimizing opportunities for physical intimacy e.g. meet outside the house at the front gate when no one is home.

3. Ask a mature and trusted friend to keep you honest through occasional questions about your relationship.

What the Bible Says...

Promise me, O women of Jerusalem,
    by the gazelles and wild deer,
    not to awaken love until the time is right.
Song of Songs 2:7, NLT

We have a little sister
    too young to have breasts.
  What will we do for our sister
    if someone asks to marry her?
  If she is a virgin, like a wall,
    we will protect her with a silver tower.
  But if she is promiscuous, like a swinging door,
    we will block her door with a cedar bar.
Song of Songs 8: 8, 9, NLT

God's will is for you to be holy, so stay away from all sexual sin. Then each of you will control his own body and live in holiness and honor— not in lustful passion like the pagans who do not know God and his ways.

1 Thessalonians 4:3-5, NLT

Your Notes...

A really intelligent man
feels what other men
only know.

- *Charles Montesquieu* [4]

Expressing Feelings

From your mother

I know you have heard me say many times that our everyday feelings are neither right nor wrong. It is what we think and how we behave that is right or wrong.

Feelings help us to enjoy life, warn us when something is wrong, and they make us human. The issue I am writing about here is one of empathy i.e. being able to put yourself in another person's shoes – feeling with another person.

We are able to feel for or feel with another person primarily because we know how we feel. If you tell me "Mummy I'm tired" I know how that feels because I have felt tired and have acknowledged that feeling in myself without rationalizing it away.

Women are normally socialized to express feelings openly. We can easily talk about being depressed, excited, rejected, afraid, unsure, happy etc. Men are not normally socialized to express how they feel but express what they think and what they do. They however do know how they feel and in a respectful environment they will share their feelings.

Where is all of this leading? Well my daughter, a

man who can only talk about his ideas, successes and actions but is unable to share how he feels from day to day may have a great problem with empathy.

You may ask what does this have to do with anything? If he is not able to identify and acknowledge his own feelings, both positive and negative, when you share that you feel lonely or tired or taken for granted he may react by minimizing what you have said or act as if he never heard you. And the reality may be that he never really heard you because of his inability to be in touch with his own feelings. This will eventually result in a breakdown of communication and leave one or both persons feeling that their needs are not being met in the marriage.

Once the inability to identify and express feelings in a respectful relationship is recognized, the couple should seek counseling to address this. Many times the person needs knowledge of the truth about feelings and to undo some of his unhealthy mindsets about feelings, which he would have learnt as a child and young person. Therefore with the help of a counsellor your intended partner can practice expressing feelings and empathy and its associated actions.

With all love and affection,

Mom

Daddy's point of view

It's amazing how in trying to distinguish men from women, we forget one powerful fact: men are still human. Men do have feelings regardless of the image they seek to project. Men experience an incredible range of emotions - happiness, excitement, anger, sadness, disappointment, anguish, fear. Our challenge however is in expressing these emotions or rather communicating how we feel to those we love.

Many women complain about their husbands being silent. "He does not say anything!" "He won't say how he feels!" Don't ever confuse failure to express feelings with not having feelings. Men DO have feelings! And they grapple with these feelings in the private arena of their minds. They internalize their concerns and feelings and unfortunately these feelings appear in a secondary form typically as anger or depression. How many times have I sought to battle these emotional gladiators in my own mental coliseum! Such battles are intense and can drain your energy and make it difficult to share how you feel or what is bothering you.

Your mother would always know when something was wrong. Obviously she asked if everything was okay with me. And what was my typical response? "I'm fine, I'm alright." Yeah right! Of course I was not alright. I may have been embarrassed, I may have felt discouraged or afraid about some situation. Maybe it was what my boss said or what a friend did. At times I was disappointed that a plan did not work out. It's easy to withdraw or react angrily with the ones we love the most. And though our loved ones are not the cause of these problems, they are the ones that bear the brunt of our emotions. This is why it is important for us men to learn how to express what we are feeling inside. Saying "I'm fine" or "It's no big deal" will not help. Left unattended, these emotions can become toxic and when finally expressed can end up hurting those who want to help us the most.

I learned that feeling a particularly way was not bad in itself. Feelings come whether we want them to or not. It's what we do with our feelings that matter. You lost your job? Its alright to feel ashamed, sad or even angry. It's what we do afterwards that's important. Will I write a nasty letter to my former employer? Will I take my anger out on my daughter? Ironically the more we share how we feel, the less likely we are to hurt those we love and we learn to express our emotions appropriately.

Your mother is wise enough to give me the space I

need to process my feelings. She is patient and does not condemn or nag me. When I am ready, she listens, helping me by providing much needed perspective. I am thankful for this and the experience has made me better at communicating how I feel not just what I say.

My prayer is that your marriage will be full of empathy and support. May your husband be understanding and self-aware, attuned to his feelings and able to express them safely and honestly. May he be sensitive to your needs and feelings as you will be to his.

Love always,

Dad

Things to Consider Before You Get Married

1. Learn and discuss the concept of emotional intelligence with your fiancé.

2. Discuss the importance of sharing your feelings with another.

3. Ask your intended partner to share a difficult time in his life with you. It could be a broken relationship, a disappointment, personal failure or conflict. Listen for the feelings expressed. Resist the temptation to be judgmental or to fix the "problem." Just listen for your friend's feelings. If your fiancé is encountering difficulty in expressing his emotions, use empathy to gently suggest the possible emotions he may have felt at that difficult time.

4. Similar to activity 3, share with your partner a difficult time in your life. How did you feel. Invite your partner to contemplate the feelings you have had. Be patient and encourage your fiancé even when the feelings suggested may be off-base.

What the Bible Says...

Then Jesus went with them to the olive grove called Gethsemane, and he said, "Sit here while I go over there to pray." He took Peter and Zebedee's two sons, James and John, and he became anguished and distressed. He told them, "My soul is crushed with grief to the point of death. Stay here and keep watch with me."

Matthew 26: 36 – 38, NLT

We think you ought to know, dear brothers and sisters, about the trouble we went through in the province of Asia. We were crushed and overwhelmed beyond our ability to endure, and we thought we would never live through it. In fact, we expected to die. But as a result, we stopped relying on ourselves and learned to rely only on God, who raises the dead.

2 Corinthians 1: 8, 9, NLT

So then, since we have a great High Priest who has entered heaven, Jesus the Son of God, let us hold firmly to what we believe. This High Priest of ours understands our weaknesses, for he faced all of the same testings we do, yet he did not sin. So let us come boldly to the throne of our gracious God. There we will receive his mercy, and we will find grace to help us when we need it most.

Hebrews 4: 14 – 16, NLT

When he [Paul] had finished speaking, he knelt and prayed with them. They all cried as they embraced and kissed him good-bye. They were sad most of all because he had said that they would never see him again. Then they escorted him down to the ship.

Acts 20: 36 – 38, NLT

Jesus had stayed outside the village, at the place where Martha met him. When the people who were at the house consoling Mary saw her leave so hastily, they assumed she was going to Lazarus's grave to weep. So they followed her there. When Mary arrived and saw Jesus, she fell at his feet and said, "Lord, if only you had been here, my brother would not have died."

When Jesus saw her weeping and saw the other people wailing with her, a deep anger welled up within him, and he was deeply troubled. "Where have you put him?" he asked them.

They told him, "Lord, come and see." **Then Jesus wept.** The people who were standing nearby said, "See how much he loved him!"

John 11: 30 – 36, NLT (emphasis added)

Your Notes...

*S*urely what a man does when he is taken off his guard is the best evidence for what sort of man he is. If there are rats in a cellar, you are most likely to see them if you go in very suddenly. But the suddenness does not create the rats: it only prevents them from hiding. In the same way the suddenness of the provocation does not make me ill tempered; it only shows me what an ill-tempered man I am.

- C. S. Lewis [5]

Anger

From your mother

Dear daughter, you know that all of us get angry. Anger is a normal emotion. Even God gets angry. Sometimes it is because of the energy of anger that we make critical yet positive changes to our lives and situations around us. Anger may be the right response when injustice or abuse confronts us, especially regarding those who are helpless and cannot defend themselves.

Some of us however, have uncontrolled or explosive anger. We seem to "trip" and overreact to everyday disappointments and human mistakes.

It is very difficult to sustain a healthy relationship with an angry man. Explosive anger is normally an indication of deep hurts especially from childhood. A person who is easily angered should get counseling to deal with the underlying causes of the anger. If the anger is not addressed it could lead to physical and verbal abuse in the relationship.

Don't make excuses for his angry outbursts. It is not you or someone else who caused him to lash out. Don't believe it when he says "If you would only stop doing X,

Y and Z, I wouldn't have to get angry and lash out this way." Or "You bring out the worst in me." He needs to own his problem and this is a serious problem. Again Proverbs says,

"Short-tempered people do foolish things…" (**14:17, NLT**).

This type of relationship will not be healthy. The man you deserve should be tenderhearted and kind, not quick to become angry or vengeful. If he submits to the leadership the Holy Spirit, the following Scripture will be true for him:

But the Holy Spirit produces this kind of fruit in our lives: love, joy, peace, patience, kindness, goodness, faithfulness, gentleness, and self-control. There is no law against these things!

Galatians 5: 22, 23, NLT

With all love and affection,

Mom

Daddy's point of view

One of my greatest challenges was dealing with anger. I was amazed at how anger lurked silently in my life only to show its ugly head at the slightest provocation. I was angry with myself, I was angry with my parents, I was angry with those who disappointed me. Unfortunately I internalised my anger and avoided expressing it to others... except your mother. It is ironic how we reveal our worst selves to ones who show us the most love. I found myself overreacting to comments or jokes made. I spoke harshly when your mother asked probing questions or expressed disagreement with my views.

I eventually discovered that my overreaction; my harsh responses were an accumulation of my past hurts and disappointments. These included parental rejections, my personal struggles with sin and my own low self esteem. Questions challenged my insecurities. I was afraid of failure or my mistakes being exposed. Anger was my ineffective way of dealing with these problems. I did not like however what I was seeing in the mirror and I dreaded a future in which anger would continue to dominate my life.

So what did I do? I prayed. I confessed my anger

problem to God. He knew about it all along and His Holy Spirit convicted me about it especially after every episode. I would hear His gentle voice speak to me as I surveyed the wreckage and damage I had done. My heart was broken as I discovered how I hurt the ones dearest to me, including you. God showed me how I could handle the situations differently and He offered me His grace and strength to remain kind and gentle. The LORD also helped me to forgive those who hurt me instead of suppressing or avoiding my feelings. This is an ongoing process but an essential one. Chronic anger, like pain, is a sign that something is wrong, unresolved. Sometimes forgiveness must be directed to ourselves. Even as I asked God to forgive me for my many sins, I needed to forgive myself.

I have also realised that unexpressed feelings can mutate into uncontrolled anger: a frustration that reveals an inability to share. This is why men should learn to share their feelings. Saying nothing is wrong when asked how we are doing is not healthy. Uncontrolled anger is dangerous and we should be careful to identify and release it to God. Ignoring your partner's anger will not help him and it will most certainly not help you. Don't make excuses for harsh outbursts that far exceed anything you might have done. Never accept physical abuse. If your partner hits you, please report it. Do not be ashamed. You did nothing wrong. You do not deserve to be hit. Speak to us. Let us know so we can help you. Some men demand that others do not get involved; that it is a private affair; that people (including parents) should respect the husband's authority. Listen to me carefully: a man forfeits that right when he hits you. I WILL get involved. We will intervene. You are our daughter and we will look out for you. Don't fool yourself. If you let it pass, if you make excuses for his abuse, it will happen again!

That's why it is important to recognize potential signs of anger issues NOW while you are courting. Encourage – no – INSIST that your friend gets help; that he shares with a counselor or mature and trusted advisor to find out how to overcome anger. Getting married to a man who cannot control his anger is like volunteering to become a suicide bomber. You are strapping explosive stuff to your life. It will only be a matter of time before the bomb goes off!

Your marriage should be an environment of peace and safety not war and sorrow. I am confident that Jesus Christ our Lord will help you to choose wisely.

Love always

Dad

Things to Consider Before You Get Married

1. Pray that God will help your friend to recognise his problem and deal with it.

2. Share your discomfort and concerns with your friend. Do not try to rationalise the problem away or accept blame for what is your friend's responsibility to deal with.

3. If you are experiencing consistent outbursts of anger from your friend, strongly encourage him to get professional help. A trained counsellor can guide him to process the source of his anger and ways to overcome it.

4. Declare your unwillingness to go forward with the relationship unless he gets help and commits to overcoming his anger problem.

What the Bible Says...

People with understanding control their anger;
    a hot temper shows great foolishness.
Proverbs 14: 29, NLT

A hot-tempered person starts fights;
    a cool-tempered person stops them.
Proverbs 15: 18, NLT

A truly wise person uses few words;
    a person with understanding is even-tempered.
Proverbs 17:27, NLT

Don't befriend angry people
    or associate with hot-tempered people,
  or you will learn to be like them
    and endanger your soul.
Proverbs 22: 24, 25, NLT

Anger is cruel, and wrath is like a flood,
>   but jealousy is even more dangerous.

Proverbs 27:4, NLT

An angry person starts fights;
>   a hot-tempered person commits all kinds of sin.

Proverbs 29: 22, NLT

When you follow the desires of your sinful nature, the results are very clear: sexual immorality, impurity, lustful pleasures, idolatry, sorcery, **hostility, quarreling, jealousy, outbursts of anger**, selfish ambition, dissension, division, envy, drunkenness, wild parties, and other sins like these. Let me tell you again, as I have before, that anyone living that sort of life will not inherit the Kingdom of God.

Galatians 5: 19 – 21, NLT (emphasis added)

"You have heard that our ancestors were told, 'You must not murder. If you commit murder, you are subject to judgment.' But I say, if you are even angry with someone, you are subject to judgment! If you call someone an idiot, you are in danger of being brought before the court. And if you curse someone, you are in danger of the fires of hell.

Matthew 5: 21, 22, NLT

And "don't sin by letting anger control you." Don't let the sun go down while you are still angry, for anger gives a foothold to the devil.

Ephesians 4: 26 – 27, NLT

But now is the time to get rid of anger, rage, malicious behavior, slander, and dirty language.

Colossians 3:8, NLT

Understand this, my dear brothers and sisters: You must all be quick to listen, slow to speak, and slow to get angry. Human anger does not produce the righteousness God desires.

James 1: 19-20, NLT

Your Notes...

*T*ell me what company you keep, and I'll tell you what you are.

- *Cervantes* [6]

His Friends

From your mother

Does he have friends? That is, are there people who he shares his life with on a meaningful level? It does not have to be a lot. One, two or three in the "inner circle" and others that he interacts with on a friendly level.

This is important because it is in these peer relationships that we learn commitment, trust, forgiveness, confidentiality, sharing and caring. A man without any friends may have problems with trust and forgiveness, which would affect your relationship. These issues must be seriously dealt with in counseling before marriage.

How about the values of his friends? Are they values that support marriage and godly principles? I have heard many women speak about their husbands having many friends before marriage. They were quite comfortable with this especially since during courting he was willing to give them (girlfriend/ fiancé) a lot of attention. After they were married, the wife was willing to allow her husband to go and "hang out with the boys." Unfortunately, these women noted with pain that he spent more time with the boys than with his family. When the wife would ask to join them in their evening or night out, he would say that it was not an environment that she would be comfortable in.

When the wives took a closer look at the lives of their husbands' friends, they noted that the friends had troubled family relationships. Such friends encouraged activities that did not promote healthy family life and sometimes activities that would actually destroy families.

True friends play an important role in family life especially by their actions and sometimes counsel. Both of you should have friends that share and live out your godly values and commitment to family. I am so thankful that God has placed a number of great friends in my life. May the Lord also bless both of you with mutual friends who are supportive and respectful of your marriage.

With all love and affection,
Mom

Daddy's point of view

I am eternally grateful to the LORD for the friends He gave me. It was these friends that helped me to process my thoughts and to desire more for myself. One of the greatest gifts a friend can bestow on you is the gift of listening. My friends listened to me as I struggled with the feelings I had for a young lovely girl who would eventually be your mother.

Another gift my friends gave me was the gift of perspective. My friends were not afraid to challenge unhealthy assumptions I held about myself, your mother, others, life or even God. I could trust them to tell me what I needed to hear. Such friends took an active interest in the success of my relationship with my wife. These men were my groomsmen and I felt protected and supported. They are men of integrity and models worthy to be followed.

Male friends are critical to a young man's development. Men impart strength and that is what so many of us need… especially from older men. My male friends hold me accountable and expect me to be a faithful husband and a loving father. I expect no less of them in their relationships.

Pay special attention to the friends of your intended partner. Take the opportunity to get to know those who seem to have the most influence with him. Pray for and encourage friendships that will challenge your intended partner to be a responsible and committed man who loves God and his wife.

Just the same, be mindful of the friends you embrace yourself. Be wary of "friends" who undermine your marriage or disrespect your husband. A healthy marriage has no place for friends who think they can usurp the intimacy between husband and wife. Ultimately you want your best friend to be your spouse.

Do not settle for anything less. You are too valuable and precious to be in competition with some friends. The man who deserves you will prioritize his relationships. He will know that you come first and he will delight to spend more time with you than with anyone else.

Love always,

Dad

Things to Consider Before You Get Married

1. Take time to get to know your fiancé's friends. Attend social or sporting events where you are likely to encounter his friends. Engage in conversation, observe their words and behaviour. Pay attention to how much influence each friend has upon your fiancé. Is it healthy? What concerns do you have?

2. Is there a strong balance of mature Christian friends in both of your lives? How frequently do both of you interact with these friends. Discuss ways you can increase these interactions.

3. Identify mature friends in each of your lives that you can both agree to approach when difficulties in your relationship cannot be solved by two of you alone.

4. Share your expectations regarding the role and interactions of friends in your relationship especially marriage. Don't assume these expectations are mutually understood or agreed to. What are your fiancé's expectations? Are you comfortable with them?

What the Bible Says...

Oh, the joys of those who do not
**   follow the advice of the wicked,**
**   or stand around with sinners,**
**   or join in with mockers.**
But they delight in the law of the Lord,
   meditating on it day and night.
They are like trees planted along the riverbank,
   bearing fruit each season.
 Their leaves never wither,
   and they prosper in all they do.
But not the wicked!
      They are like worthless chaff, scattered by the
wind.
   They will be condemned at the time of judgment.
   Sinners will have no place among the godly.
For the Lord watches over the path of the godly,
   but the path of the wicked leads to destruction.
Psalm 1, NLT (emphasis added)

Walk with the wise and become wise;
    associate with fools and get in trouble.
Proverbs 13:20, NLT

My child, listen and be wise:
    Keep your heart on the right course.
  Do not carouse with drunkards
    or feast with gluttons,
for they are on their way to poverty,
    and too much sleep clothes them in rags.
Listen to your father, who gave you life,
    and don't despise your mother when she is old.
Proverbs 23: 19 - 22, NLT

There are "friends" who destroy each other,
    but a real friend sticks closer than a brother.
Proverbs 18: 24, NLT

Don't envy evil people

or desire their company.

For their hearts plot violence,

and their words always stir up trouble.

Proverbs 24: 1, 2, NLT

…"Let's feast and drink, for tomorrow we die!" Don't be fooled by those who say such things, for "bad company corrupts good character."

1 Corinthians 15: 32, 33, NLT

Your Notes...

He who asks is a fool for five minutes, but he who does not ask remains a fool forever.

- Chinese Proverb [7]

Seeking Help

From your mother

Y ou know I would say that no one knows everything and we all know this is true. As a result, from time to time we will encounter situations and problems that will require the help of others to overcome or resolve.

Even in relationships we may need help or counsel to resolve or get a different perspective on our problem. It is important that you are both willing to receive counsel. In some families there is a culture of "we can work it out on our own, we don't need outside help." The result is that the couple fights between themselves for years and nothing improves.

Receiving help, especially for a man, may make him feel inadequate, vulnerable and less of a man. This is understandable, however being willing to receive outside help that is wise, mature and confidential is a prerequisite for a healthy marriage because you may need it.

A number of women have told me that their husbands would never go for counseling. When I ask if there is anyone in his family or circle of friends and colleagues that he respects and would listen to, they would despairingly state that he listens to no one. Some would even say that if he knew that she was speaking to me right now that he would be very angry. One can feel their pain and loneliness.

A heart that is open to counsel is a heart that will also be open to what the Holy Spirit has to say. Let us remember that the Holy Spirit may use individuals to speak through. Again Proverbs says:

"Where there is no counsel, the people fail;

But in the multitude of counselors there is safety." **(11:14, NKJV)**

With all love and affection,

Mom

Daddy's point of view

Seeking the help of others is not a sign of weakness but demonstrates both humility and strength. Thankfully I learned early in my relationship that I did not have all the answers. As a result I benefitted from the wisdom of diverse sources for various situations. For example, your grandparents helped us tremendously during your mother's pregnancy and after you were born. Parenting can be difficult even overwhelming for those who are experiencing it for the first time. If I was arrogant to believe that we did not need assistance, we might have risked terrible stress upon our marriage.

There was also the time when we had to live at your grandparents' home for awhile. Initially I felt uncomfortable about this, even a little embarrassed and ashamed. I always envisioned providing for my family and that included a place to stay. But we are not always in control of our circumstances and at that particular time we could not afford to pay a higher rent. So we asked for permission to move back home with your mother's parents. I remember about a day after we moved in, I was just sitting in front of our television and staring for hours. I felt out of sorts, out of place but thankfully your grandparents were full of grace. They never made me uncomfortable and respected our space even though we lived in their house. We eventually decided that we would stay there until we purchased our own home. Renting can be a stressful experience in our country and we felt that the money used for rent would be better served by paying a mortgage. I came to realize that the real definition of rent is "paying another person's mortgage with interest!" Thankfully in our fifth year, we were able to purchase our own home. This would not have been possible if your grandparents did not accommodate us as they did.

Our predisposition to seek help in difficult times was not accidental. During our courtship we agreed on the persons we could go to should we need assistance. These persons are mutual friends that we respect and we have given one another the freedom to access their counsel. I am quite comfortable with my wife seeking advice from her parents. And although such advice is given, we agree that the final decision is ours to make. We want to have the best possible information to make critical decisions and this requires us to be open to others. The moment we cut others off from sharing from their knowledge, wisdom and experience we are setting ourselves up for eventual failure.

Don't admire the man who prides himself in not needing others to help him. Be afraid, be very afraid.

Would a drowning man refuse the help of a lifeguard or any other person for that matter? We would consider that drowning man to be a fool not a hero. Why then do we attribute strength to someone who fails to seek help when they are unable to solve problems on their own?

Finally, continue to be a blessing to others. Remember to help those who are less fortunate. Don't be stingy. Be a giver. Let the Lord show you how your marriage can a blessing to those around you. Give and it shall be given to you (Luke 6: 38). Show mercy and you will receive mercy (James 2: 13).

Love always,

Dad

Things to Consider Before You Get Married

1. Discuss the importance of enlisting others to help you both in event of difficult relational conflict.

2. Agree on a list of family and friends that each of you can approach when the need arises.

3. Begin talking to these individuals about various areas that you need information about. Get comfortable NOW with discussing issues with them. It could be as simple as asking advice for choice of appliances or intimate tips for your honeymoon. The point is to develop the lines of communication so when crises happen, it will not be strange for you to seek their help.

4. Pray together about matters that you are concerned about. After all prayer is a way of seeking help. God is our ultimate Helper and we should develop the habit of inviting Him into our affairs. Too many couples seek to solve problems in their own wisdom and strength. Your Heavenly Father gladly wants you to ask Him for help. Don't ignore this awesome privilege.

What the Bible Says...

People who accept discipline are on the pathway to life,

but those who ignore correction will go astray.

Proverbs 10: 17, NLT

Without wise leadership, a nation falls;

there is safety in having many advisers.

Proverbs 11: 14, NLT

Fools think their own way is right,

but the wise listen to others.

Proverbs 12: 15, NLT

Haughtiness goes before destruction;

humility precedes honor.

Proverbs 18: 12, NLT

Trust in the Lord with all your heart;
do not depend on your own understanding.
Seek his will in all you do,
and he will show you which path to take.
Proverbs 3: 5, 6, NLT

"And so I tell you, keep on asking, and you will receive what you ask for. Keep on seeking, and you will find. Keep on knocking, and the door will be opened to you. For everyone who asks, receives. Everyone who seeks, finds. And to everyone who knocks, the door will be opened.

"You fathers—if your children ask for a fish, do you give them a snake instead? Or if they ask for an egg, do you give them a scorpion? Of course not! So if you sinful people know how to give good gifts to your children, how much more will your heavenly Father give the Holy Spirit to those who ask him."
Luke 11: 9 – 13, NLT

I look up to the mountains—
does my help come from there?
My help comes from the Lord,
who made heaven and earth!
Psalm 121: 1, 2, NLT

Your Notes...

*H*ow many times have your parents told you not to do things, and the next thing you know, you go do it? And you realized you shouldn't have done it.

- Michael Jordan 8

Parental Wisdom

From your mother

My dear child, I have come to realize that in addition to using parents to bring us into the world, God gives them, regardless of their religious and educational backgrounds, insight into the suitability of the people around us especially our marriage partner.

I have heard women say in tears that one or both of their parents did not approve of their choice for various reasons and now that things are going badly, they are afraid to let their parents know because they warned them.

Most parents are forgiving of their children and would be supportive of them through these difficulties. What you get from all of this is the importance of listening to the views of your parents, close family and friends concerning your choice.

We say that "love is blind" so there may be things that you may not see or don't want to see. You may even think that your love for him may change certain negative things. Please strongly consider the concerns of others regarding your marital choice.

There are cosmetic concerns like "he's too skinny"

(I got that with your father), "too dark", "too tall" or "too short". These are not the concerns I am referring to. There are rather, deeper concerns about his temperament and attitude, values, ambition, work ethic and commitment to Jesus. In other words, what is his character like? Remember, character always trumps physical appearance.

If these concerns arise and they are not addressed and you do get married you are in for some very painful and turbulent times.

With all love and affection,

Mom

Daddy's point of view

You know that my grandparents raised me. So it was their wisdom I relied on while growing up and making the transition into adulthood and relationships. I was fortunate that they were still alive when I met your mother. I eventually invited your mother to meet with them. With that twinkle in her eyes, my grandmother gave her approval after talking with your mother.

Meeting your mother's parents for the first time made me very nervous but is was essential. I was mindful that I was being observed and I definitely wanted to make a good impression. Your mother always spoke highly and affectionately about her parents and siblings and it became clear to me that she valued the opinion and wisdom of her family. Call it strategy, common sense or simply manners, but I took care to respectfully address her parents, hold conversations with them, and answer questions they may ask. I respected and observed any rules they had for their home and family. I dared not encourage your mother to disobey her parents and I honoured any time limits placed on my visits.

Early in our relationship, your grandmother asked your mother to limit our times together. Your grandmother was initially not too thrilled with our relationship and concerned that we were getting too close too soon. Obviously we were unhappy with this instruction (people in love usually are) but I felt it was important to honour her mother's request. As a man and a follower of Christ it was important that I led by example and be a person of integrity even when things did not go my way. I would not be a wedge between your mother and her family. And I trusted that the LORD would honour this decision and work it out however He pleased. And He did.

Today I have a great relationship with your grandparents. I have already shared how your grandparents helped us tremendously when we needed a place to stay. I have also been blessed by their wisdom and insight. Being able to share concerns or thoughts about a particular issue, whether at work or home, with my mother-in-law was a great comfort to me. I knew that she would share advice that was trustworthy and most importantly in line with the character of Christ. And if she did not know what to say, she would pray. That was good enough for me.

Be wary of any man who makes fun of your relationship with your parents, or wants to encourage you to disobey or dishonour your mother and father. You know fully well that honoring your parents is an important criteria for receiving God's blessing of a long and quality life.

You have already shown yourself to be wise. You have been respectful and courteous. You have made your mother and I very proud. We are confident that you will continue to do what pleases the Lord.

Love always,

Dad

Things to Consider Before You Get Married

1. Once you believe there is a serious possibility of a relationship, discuss it with your parents. Welcome their questions, wisdom and advice.

2. Insist on your friend meeting with your parents as well as you meeting with his parents/ guardians.

3. Inform one another of rules and instructions that your parents require you to follow. Respect these requirements and help each other to keep them.

4. Make a commitment to help one another honour your parents. Let your friend know that you are serious about honoring your parents and that you believe parental honour is tied to God's blessing for your life.

5. Keep your parents informed regarding challenges or concerns you may have about your relationship. You may benefit greatly from their input.

What the Bible Says...

Children, obey your parents because you belong to the Lord, for this is the right thing to do. "Honor your father and mother." This is the first commandment with a promise: If you honor your father and mother, "things will go well for you, and you will have a long life on the earth."

Ephesians 6: 1 – 3, NLT

My child, listen when your father corrects you.

Don't neglect your mother's instruction.

What you learn from them will crown you with grace and be a chain of honor around your neck.

Proverbs 1: 8, 9, NLT

My son, obey your father's commands,

and don't neglect your mother's instruction.

Keep their words always in your heart.

Tie them around your neck.

When you walk, their counsel will lead you.

When you sleep, they will protect you.

When you wake up, they will advise you.

For their command is a lamp

and their instruction a light;

their corrective discipline

is the way to life.

Proverbs 6: 20 – 23, NLT

People who despise advice are asking for trouble;

those who respect a command will succeed.

The instruction of the wise is like a life-giving fountain;

those who accept it avoid the snares of death.

Proverbs 13: 13, 14, NLT

Your Notes...

*H*ere is an unabashed quotation from John H. Adam and Nancy Williamson Adam: "Letting go of your marriage—if it is no longer a good one—can be the most successful thing you have ever done. Getting a divorce can be a positive, problem-solving, growth-orientated step. It can be a personal triumph." Here is the secular mind in all its shameless perversity. It celebrates failure as success, disintegration as growth, and disaster as triumph.

- John Stott [9]

About Divorce

From your mother

Dear daughter,

This is just a note. It concerns marrying a divorced man. There are many different views on this and you know how your father and I feel about this and our understanding on this issue.

I know that you would not be the only one reading this letter so I want to say to other women as well that a divorce indicates that there are issues which were unresolved.

It is important for one to get professional counseling and be very open about the past relationship and one's role in the breakdown of the relationship. Note that in the marriage both persons are responsible for the breakdown and ultimately divorce. Be very careful and cautious in these waters. I would prefer that you do not marry a divorced person.

Also getting into a relationship with someone who just broke off from a committed relationship less than one year ago is very risky and is not advisable.

With all love and affection,

Mom

Daddy's point of view

Divorce is a very painful experience. One I would not wish for you. Divorce is more than the annulling of a legal contract. It is not just a parting of ways. Divorce is breaking a covenant made before both God and human witnesses. And because the both of you will become one flesh through the mystery of marriage, divorce is also an amputation! Consider if you went to a doctor because your hand had an infection. She examines you thoughtfully and makes her diagnosis. She tells you that you can treat this infection by antibiotics or you can have an operation to amputate the hand so that the infection does not spread to the rest of your body. What would you do? You'd likely take the antibiotics! Why? Because your hand is precious to you. You would also be severely limited for the rest of your life.

It is no different with divorce and in some cases it's actually worse. Think about the emotions of betrayal and abandonment you will encounter. To have shared your life with someone so intimately and then for the person to no longer be there and even worse for that person to marry someone else! That's why many divorced women see divorce as a type of death. But the grieving is different. It's a silent grieving in which there is no ceremony, there is no closure and there are few mourners. The object of your grief still lives, still walks and moves on with his life.

And if you have children they will be terribly affected as well. Some children carry a heavy burden of misplaced guilt believing that they are the reason their parent are getting divorced. Many children who experience divorce suffer emotionally and academically. And in some unfortunate cases, children are made to choose between parents. This should not be! You will most likely also seek custody for your children thus increasing your financial burden since you will be relying on your source of income alone.

So how do you escape the painful amputation of divorce? How do you ensure that you do not become another statistic? Another 29 year old divorcee? Unfortunately there are no guarantees and in some cases it will happen. You cannot force someone to stay with you. And that is why you need to choose your marriage partner wisely. To choose someone who believes that divorce is an option or for whom marriage is merely a contract rather than a holy covenant made with you and God before witnesses is to court potential disaster. My dear child, hear me carefully: Do not enter into a relationship with someone who sees divorce as an option if things go wrong. Because things WILL go wrong. Why should you have the cloud of divorce perpetually hanging over your head?

If both of you share the core value that divorce is not an option; that God hates divorce, you will have a greater chance of overcoming marriage failure. Now resisting divorce does not mean that you ignore the problems plaguing your marriage. No! You will seek help. If your safety is at stake you may have to remove yourself for a period until there is real change. But the intention of the temporary separation should be clear to all: it is to facilitate healing and reconciliation. Separation is NOT a stage closer to divorce, as many practice it today. Separation, if needed, is designed to be U-turn to a better marriage. What you do during this period of separation is absolutely vital. You will need to involve those persons you both agreed to turn to in times of crisis. You will need to get counselling. You will need the grace of God to take you through this.I pray that you will never have to experience divorce. This is one of the main reasons, your mother and I have written this book. We want you to have a great marriage; to enjoy life with your spouse; to grow old together; to leave a beautiful legacy for your children and generations to come.

This is our hope for you. May the Lord keep you for the person He has prepared for you: a man after God's heart; a man who is confident yet humble; strong yet tender; self-aware yet selfless. May the Lord bless you with a husband who cherishes you as his own body. May the man that captures your heart be so ravished with your beauty that he becomes satisfied with your love and your love alone. May the Lord make both of you into a powerful ministry that blesses generations and causes those who are downtrodden to rejoice. May your marriage accurately reflect the love and passion that exists between Christ and His Church.

Love always,

Dad

Things to Consider Before You Get Married

1. Read and discuss with your intended partner, the Scriptures relating to divorce in the following section.

2. Ask your intended partner about their views and position on divorce. Are you comfortable with his position? Are his views compatible with yours?

3. Share with your intended partner, your views and expectations regarding divorce

4. Brainstorm the true costs of divorce to spouses and children.

5. Discuss with your intended partner strategies for reducing the risk of divorce to your marriage.

6. Agree on persons and other resources that you can access to help bring healing to your marriage in times of crisis.

What the Bible Says...

Here is another thing you do. You cover the Lord's altar with tears, weeping and groaning because he pays no attention to your offerings and doesn't accept them with pleasure. You cry out, "Why doesn't the Lord accept my worship?" I'll tell you why! Because the Lord witnessed the vows you and your wife made when you were young. But you have been unfaithful to her, though she remained your faithful partner, the wife of your marriage vows.

Didn't the Lord make you one with your wife? In body and spirit you are his. And what does he want? Godly children from your union. So guard your heart; remain loyal to the wife of your youth. **"For I hate divorce!" says the Lord, the God of Israel.** "To divorce your wife is to overwhelm her with cruelty," says the Lord of Heaven's Armies. "So guard your heart; do not be unfaithful to your wife."

Malachi 2: 13 – 16, NLT (emphasis added).

"You have heard the law that says, 'A man can divorce his wife by merely giving her a written notice of divorce.' But I say that a man who divorces his wife, unless she has been unfaithful, causes her to commit adultery. And anyone who marries a divorced woman also commits adultery.

Matthew 5: 31, 32, NLT

Some Pharisees came and tried to trap him with this question: "Should a man be allowed to divorce his wife?"

Jesus answered them with a question: "What did Moses say in the law about divorce?"

"Well, he permitted it," they replied. "He said a man can give his wife a written notice of divorce and send her away."

But Jesus responded, "He wrote this commandment only as a concession to your hard hearts. But 'God made them male and female' from the beginning of creation. 'This explains why a man leaves his father and mother and is joined to his wife, and the two are united into one.' Since they are no longer two but one, let no one split apart what God has joined together."

Later, when he was alone with his disciples in the house, they brought up the subject again. He told them, "Whoever divorces his wife and marries someone else commits adultery against her. And if a woman divorces her husband and marries someone else, she commits adultery."

Mark 10: 2 – 12, NLT

But for those who are married, I have a command that comes not from me, but from the Lord. A wife must not leave her husband. But if she does leave him, let her remain single or else be reconciled to him. And the husband must not leave his wife.

1 Corinthians 7: 10, 11, NLT

As the Scriptures say, "A man leaves his father and mother and is joined to his wife, and the two are united into one." **This is a great mystery, but it is an illustration of the way Christ and the church are one.** So again I say, each man must love his wife as he loves himself, and the wife must respect her husband.

Ephesians 5: 31 – 33, NLT (emphasis added).

Your Notes...

Spiritual togetherness is only possible through the work of the Holy Spirit. If we have been set apart by the Spirit, He resides in our life. The result is a mysterious union with Christ, and with those who know Him as Savior. So if we want to grow closer spiritually, we must make sure that each of us has a saving relationship with God through faith in Christ.

- L. A. Ferrebee [10]

Becoming Unequally Yoked

From your mother

Dear daughter,

Can two walk together unless they agree (**Amos 3:3**)? This question asked by the prophet Amos over two thousand years ago is obviously relevant for any marriage. I want to look at the issue of being unequally yoked from a values perspective. Your values are principles that inform your behaviour. All of us have core values, that is values that are non-negotiable. These are values we are not willing to change and they should be present in the people we choose to have deep and healthy relationships with.

Your father and I share the following core values:

God must be the first priority

Family life is very important

Our lives must be examples that others can follow

Helping others is part of our mission in life

Honesty

Faithfulness

Everyone is important and priceless

Do unto others as you would have them do unto you

One must try to obey God in all things

One's values must be seen in one's behaviour. Anyone can say that they are honest but does he show honesty in his daily interactions with others? Will he be honest even if he knows you or others would become angry with him? You see 'talk is cheap' and we can't just take a person's word about what is important to them or what they believe. You will know what a person believes by the way he/she lives. Matthew 7:16 says "You can identify them by their fruit, that is, by the way they act. Can you pick grapes from thornbushes, or figs from thistles?"

If you choose to marry someone with different core values (unequally yoked) you will be setting yourself up for endless conflicts and eventual disappointment and heartache. You may not value everything in the same way (e.g. food tastes, sports) and that is alright but your core values should be similar.

With all love and affection,
Mom

Daddy's point of view

As we have earlier stated, your two most important decisions are whom you will serve and whom you will marry. Your relationship with the Lord Jesus Christ overshadows and transforms all other relationships. Jesus is our Supreme Desire, our Greatest Attraction. No person, no treasure, no fear, or promise can compare with the beauty, character and person of our Lord and Saviour. He gave all so that we could enjoy all things for all eternity. He gave His life so that we may have life. How foolish it would be then to forsake Him and His wonderful promises to us!

This is why it is also important that the man you marry also loves and serves Jesus Christ. Note that I did not say that this man must be someone who merely "goes to church" or "knows about God." Sadly, there are many men who perform religious duties but in their hearts they are not interested in serving the Lord or becoming like Him. Some men would even attend church services just to impress or fool you into thinking that they are spiritual. Be very careful!

Also don't be impressed by the man who appears to be knowledgeable about the Bible or theology. While knowing the Holy Scriptures are important, it is even more vital that you observe how that man is allowing the Bible to transform and direct his life. What you want to examine is the man's character - how his devotion to God is demonstrated in other relationships. Again you are looking for evidence of the fruit of the Spirit in the man's life. As a Christian, is this man consistently demonstrating and increasing in:

love,

joy,

peace,

patience,

kindness,

goodness,

faithfulness,

gentleness, and

self-control? (**Galatians 5: 22, 23, NLT**)

Or is he constantly expressing, even defending actions of:

sexual immorality,

impurity,

lustful pleasures,

idolatry,

sorcery,

hostility,

quarreling,

jealousy,

outbursts of anger,

selfish ambition,

dissension,

division,

envy,

drunkenness,

wild parties,

and other sins like these? (**Galatians 5: 19 – 21, NLT**)

The verdict on such people according to the Scriptures is clear:

"Let me tell you again, as I have before, that anyone living that sort of life will not inherit the Kingdom of God." (**Galatians 5: 21, NLT**).

Now God's intention is that your marriage will reflect

Jesus' relationship with the church. It is a relationship in which both parties are of the same mind and share the same passion: to glorify God, to facilitate His Will. How can this be done if you are married to someone who is not committed to the LORD like yourself?

Please do not fall into the trap of believing that you can eventually lead your friend to Christ and therefore have a relationship with him. There are two reasons why this is not a wise decision. First, your friend may see Jesus as a means to an end - you! Your friend may do this simply because he knows this is what you want. Now, some men have made genuine commitments to Christ in such circumstances. But this is not the norm. Second, if and when your friend becomes a Christian, he is a babe in Christ compared to you. He will need discipleship and he will be learning to put on Christ while at the same time putting off his former life. Both of you will be at different stages in your walk with God. Such a gap can present an incredible strain on a relationship in which the man is spiritually immature. As a woman, you will expect and yearn for your husband to lead, to hear God and provide direction in the home. Are you confident; can you guarantee that an immature Christian will rise to this challenge? Are you prepared to wait for this to happen? Will it ever happen? Some men in such a situation have either stopped serving Jesus or are satisfied with remaining babes in Christ. Both scenarios will leave you filled with regret.

I remember, when I was much younger, discussing with a good friend a mutual desire to lead someone of the opposite sex to Christ. I don't know why we thought about doing this. It was simply an innocent desire to experience sharing Christ with girls (after all we both went to an all-male school). Well the Lord did answer our prayer and in our first year at University, we had the glorious privilege of presenting Christ to not one but at least four girls. Two of them gave their lives to the Lord! And we were absolutely thrilled. But there was just one problem. These girls were extremely attractive and being young men we conducted a… ahem… "feasibility assessment." Should we pursue possible relationships with them? Well, we thought about it very deeply and we came to an obvious conclusion. To seek a romantic relationship would jeopardize the most important relationship these girls were now developing - their relationship with Jesus. We definitely did not want to get between these girls and Christ. We decided to remain brothers and examples of what it meant to follow Christ. At first it was very challenging but the Lord gave us the grace. We also discovered as time passed, that the difference in spiritual maturity would have posed a problem for any romantic relationship. One may look at this as a lost opportunity but the

Lord honoured our decision and has since blessed us both with beautiful and spiritually mature wives.

Ultimately my dear daughter, it boils down to trust. Do we really believe that the Lord will connect us with the person that we need? Do we trust that God is actively concerned, even setting up that divine encounter with our future spouse? We have learned to trust God for so many things from the mundane (money to pay a bill) to the critical (healing from a life threatening disease). Should we not also trust Him to bring us together with a spouse that also loves Jesus and is passionate about His kingdom?

Like Ruth, I encourage you to continue working in the Lord's Harvest. Focus on serving Him. Eventually you will capture the attention of the one who will be your blessed husband. Already he may be observing you, taking note of your faithfulness and compassion. Already the Lord may be setting both of you up for a healthy and enjoyable marriage. Wait on the Lord my dear child. Commit your desire for a secure marriage into God's hands. You will not be disappointed.

Love always,

Dad

Things to Consider Before You Get Married

1. Read the book of Ruth. Ask the Lord to give you insight and understanding regarding this powerful account in the Bible. Examine Ruth's attitude towards relationships. Take a closer look at the characters of Naomi, Ruth and Boaz. What do each of them tell you about people and relationships? What can you learn from them? Consider how God uses circumstances to bring us into our purpose and calling?

2. Commit the process of meeting the right person into the Lord's hands. Ask the Lord to give you the strength to resist the temptation of getting into a relationship with someone who is attractive but does not know Jesus. Regularly confess your confidence in God's ability to connect you with a suitable marriage partner. Inform interested men that you will not get into a relationship with someone who is not passionately following Jesus.

3. Carefully examine your friend's profession of faith. Ask your friend to share with you how he came to follow Christ. Is he speaking merely about going to church or being "born" into

church? Do you observe a passion or excitement in him when you mention Jesus and the gospel? Is there a recognition of his need for God's grace? Does he put confidence in his own deeds to gain favour with God? Is your friend concerned about the spiritual condition of others? How does he demonstrate his commitment to Jesus? What is his reputation amongst believers and unbelievers? Ask other people about him.

4. Co-develop a Marriage Mission. Discuss and draft together with your intended marriage partner, a statement that describes the kind of marriage you desire and how both of you will work together to be a blessing to others. Consider the gifts and talents God has given both of you. Examine opportunities that facilitate the complementary use of your knowledge, experience, gifts and talents. Ask, "Who can benefit from our marriage?" Please remember that other young people are desperately looking for healthy marriages for encouragement and examples to follow.

What the Bible Says...

Do not be yoked together with unbelievers. For what do righteousness and wickedness have in common? Or what fellowship can light have with darkness? What harmony is there between Christ and Belial? What does a believer have in common with an unbeliever? What agreement is there between the temple of God and idols? For we are the temple of the living God. As God has said: "I will live with them and walk among them, and I will be their God, and they will be my people."

2 Corinthians 6: 14 – 16, NIV

King Solomon, however, loved many foreign women besides Pharaoh's daughter—Moabites, Ammonites, Edomites, Sidonians and Hittites. They were from nations about which the Lord had told the Israelites, "You must not intermarry with them, because they will surely turn your hearts after their gods." Nevertheless, Solomon held fast to them in love. He had seven hundred wives of royal birth and three hundred concubines, and his wives led him astray. As Solomon grew old, his wives turned his heart after other gods, and his heart was not fully devoted to the Lord his God, as the heart of David his father had been. He followed Ashtoreth the goddess of the Sidonians, and Molek the detestable god of the Ammonites. So Solomon did evil in the eyes of the Lord; he did not follow the Lord completely, as David his father had done.

1 Kings 11: 1 – 6, NIV

Your Notes...

A Father's Letter to Young Men

Dear young man,

I am writing to you because you have shown some interest in my daughter. You have expressed your intentions to marry her and I think it is only fitting that you understand what my expectations are for any young man seeking my daughter's hand. I find myself in an ironic position having been a young man who once nervously asked my girlfriend's father for permission to marry her. Now having a daughter, I can appreciate the significance of the occasion as well as the fear and trepidation it brings. Now some men may claim that they are not nervous, that this experience is no big deal. Well, I do not care for such men coming around my daughter and I definitely hope you are not one of them! After all this is a very important milestone in your life. You are offering to assume responsibility for God's precious gift in my life; you are declaring your willingness to care for someone very dear to my wife and I. This is indeed a sacred trust and to be nervous about approaching us is a sign of your appreciation of how serious our daughter's future is to us.

But I am getting ahead of myself. Let us talk about you - you, even before you ever got to know my daughter. Even then the Lord was preparing you for this moment. You see, many men go into relationships hoping that a woman will make them whole. They are sorely wrong! Only God can make us whole. And when we miss this point we place unfair burdens and expectations on others to fulfill. Some of us would have been hurt or disappointed by parents or previous loves but unless we forgive, unless we allow God to heal our hurts, we will likely hurt others in the future. This is why it is so important to deal with the reality of your past now! Share your struggles or fears with someone who can give you wise and mature counsel. Be honest about your feelings and talk to God; listen to what the Holy Spirit is saying to you and obey what He tells you to do.

As men we should understand that God takes us through a process of development. It's a lifelong process involving success, failure, hard lessons, key friendships, times alone, discipline, critical self-reflection and self-awareness, faith, doubt, equipping, and hopefully wisdom - deep wisdom. Through these experiences we get to know about ourselves and how important it is to depend on God. Indeed, God uses these life experiences to build character in us. We soon discover that our wholeness, hope and satisfaction comes from loving and serving the Lord Jesus Christ. And it is this relationship with Jesus that is the source of our power, our strength, our wisdom, our love and blessings to others. So please remember that the first and most important asset you could ever offer my daughter is your love and commitment to the Lord Jesus Christ.

Why is following Jesus most important? Because our Lord Jesus demonstrated for us the ultimate expression of love: laying down our lives for those dear to us (John 15: 13). He expressed his love for his bride (the Church) by giving his life for us (Ephesians 5: 25 – 33). So if you're going to truly love my daughter, you will need to allow God's love to flow through you to her daily. Please do not neglect your relationship with Jesus or worse - pretend to have a relationship with Jesus so you can impress our daughter. You will be doing a great disservice to yourself as a man and God's creation.

My next expectation is that you are a man of integrity, a man of your word. There are too many men who use words to charm, persuade, and entice. They talk "love" but their actions betray self-centeredness and insensitivity. Such men overpromise when courting and under-deliver after they are married. Like dishonest used car salesmen, they will do anything to get the sale but are nowhere to be found when the car gives problems. Marriage is not a game. It's not a simple contract in which there is some escape clause you can use when things do not go well. Marriage requires character and part of that character involves keeping your vows. There is a growing trend for couples to customize their wedding vows. But what good are fancy words if you do not honour their intent. Do not be like the weak and unprincipled "men" who would abandon their vows because their wives are no longer physically desirable or because of some petty disagreement. If you are ever tempted to forsake your vows, remember the many witnesses who were there on that special day. Remember the example you will be leaving for your children to follow. One of the most powerful blessings you can give to your children is a loving and healthy marriage.

Guard your heart well, persevere, resist temptation. Marriage does not make you blind or impervious to other women. In fact some women may pursue you because you are married. This is where your commitment to refrain from sex until you are married will prove helpful. Such a commitment develops the discipline to resist future temptation. Let your wife be your shield. Do not flirt with other women. Inform your wife of any attractions you may feel to other women and let her be aware of your movements. Do not exclude your wife from your social networks. Very important, let others have no doubt about your love and commitment to your wife. While other men may be struggling to save their marriage, be mindful that a healthy and loving marriage will save you. It will protect you, it will develop you and it will promote you.

My final expectation - rather prayer is that you will be a man of grace. We are all daily recipients of God's mercy, grace and forgiveness. Nothing is as light and beautiful as a soul that is redeemed; that is forgiven. Nothing is as ugly and fearful than the soul that constantly withholds forgiveness. This is why it is important to allow God to deliver us from our past. How many men are angry and bitter because of hurt and disappointment? A vulnerable son abandoned by his father. A boy regularly abused, or ridiculed by his mother. Such experiences threaten to repeat themselves as hurting boys become hurting men. As the saying goes, "Hurt people hurt people." If we are going to break this deadly cycle we will need to forgive and release those who have hurt us. Do not be fooled. If you actively harbour bitterness and anger in your heart, your intended wife and future family will suffer for it. Unforgiveness will deform you into a vessel incapable of extending grace and mercy to others. If you are wise, you will soon realise that forgiveness is for your sake as much as it is for the offender. Forgiving others is to release yourself from the poison of the offense.

Being a man of grace is also to extend grace and mercy to others. It means that you will forgive your wife when she makes mistakes. In grace you will seek forgiveness when you are wrong and you will be humble and gentle when you are right. Grace compensates for our shortcomings and love indeed covers a multitude of sins. Do not remain angry, be quick to reconcile. And just as your heavenly Father has forgiven you, be ever so willing to forgive and restore your wife. And remember the wisdom of the Scriptures:

Love prospers when a fault is forgiven,

But dwelling on it separates close friends.

Proverbs 17: 9, NLT

As I said when I began this letter, I battled with fears and wondered if I had what it took to take responsibility for another man's daughter. Would I honour my vows? Would I be a loving husband and a caring father? Would this woman regret marrying me? Though such thoughts can sober us, it is not enough to focus on them to the point of doubt and hopelessness. Such fears and concerns should lead us to seek the LORD's help daily; to humbly accept His grace in our time of need and shun any semblance of arrogance that may creep into us because of small achievements or feeble praise heaped upon us. If you trust in Jesus, he will give you the ability to be a powerful blessing to your future family.

I strongly encourage you to read the rest of this book so that you will know what our expectations are for our precious daughter. To do so would further demonstrate your love for our daughter and your respect for her parents. As responsible parents we also encourage both of you to commit to premarital counselling. Don't be like others who see such counselling as a mere formality or a grudging obligation. It is one of the most valuable steps you can take in ensuring a healthy and successful marriage.

We look forward to hearing your plans and how we can help you prepare for your future. No doubt we will also talk together as men. I will be happy to share my own experiences in courtship and marriage. Please do not hesitate to call me or to ask questions.

Best regards,

Father to a precious princess.

About the Authors

Huey and Petreece Cuffie have each been followers of Jesus Christ for over twenty years. They have been married for sixteen years and have a lovely daughter Joelle who is twelve years old.

Huey and Petreece work extensively with young people helping them to develop their leadership, relational and vocational effectiveness. As part of their Marriage Mission, they have a deep desire to see couples have fulfilling marriages! To this end, they facilitate premarital and healthy marriage workshops.

Petreece is the author of the premarital resource, Preparing for a Successful Marriage. She is a professional counsellor with over eighteen years counselling experience. She has counselled and helped hundreds of individuals, couples and families. Petreece was the head Counsellor of the Rape Crisis Society where she dealt with many domestic violence cases.

Huey Cuffie holds a Masters in Leadership from Walden University. Huey is the co-host of the men's radio programme called MenTalk, which airs on Saturdays on ISAAC 98.1 FM. He works with men in mentoring and training

Huey and Petreece are both graduates of the University of the West Indies where they first met. Huey and Petreece own and run the Counselling and Consulting Firm, Petreece Cuffie and Associates located in El Dorado, Trinidad and Tobago.

References

1 Water, M. (2000). The new encyclopedia of Christian quotations (p. 374). Alresford, Hampshire: John Hunt Publishers Ltd.

2 Zuck, R. B. (1997). The speaker's quote book: over 4,500 illustrations and quotations for all occasions (p. 150). Grand Rapids, MI: Kregel Publications.

3 Water, M. (2000). The new encyclopedia of Christian quotations (p. 942). Alresford, Hampshire: John Hunt Publishers Ltd.

4 Water, M. (2000). The new encyclopedia of Christian quotations (p. 305). Alresford, Hampshire: John Hunt Publishers Ltd.

5 Zuck, R. B. (1997). The speaker's quote book: over 4,500 illustrations and quotations for all occasions (p. 14). Grand Rapids, MI: Kregel Publications.

6 Water, M. (2000). The new encyclopedia of Christian quotations (p. 384). Alresford, Hampshire: John Hunt Publishers Ltd.

7 Water, M. (2000). The new encyclopedia of Christian quotations (p. 516). Alresford, Hampshire: John Hunt Publishers Ltd.

8 http://articles.latimes.com/2003/apr/13/sports/sp-dogjordan13

9 Water, M. (2000). The new encyclopedia of Christian quotations (pp. 285–286). Alresford, Hampshire: John Hunt Publishers Ltd.

10 Ferrebee, L. A. (2001). The healthy marriage handbook (p. 166). Nashville, TN: Broadman & Holman Publishers.

www.ingramcontent.com/pod-product-compliance
Lightning Source LLC
LaVergne TN
LVHW051134080426
835510LV00018B/2404